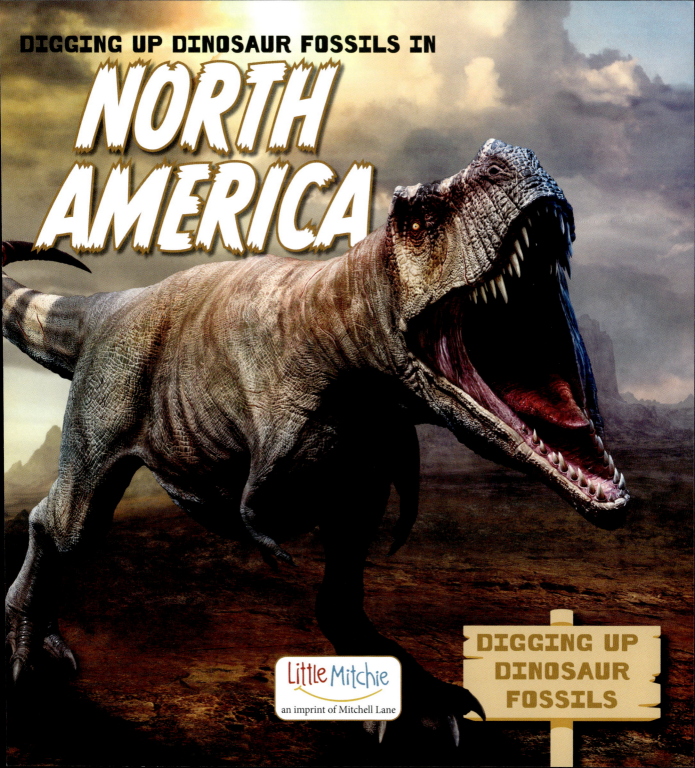
DIGGING UP DINOSAUR FOSSILS IN NORTH AMERICA

Little Mitchie
an imprint of Mitchell Lane

DIGGING UP DINOSAUR FOSSILS

Creating Young Nonfiction Readers

Little Mitchie lets children delve into nonfiction at beginning reading levels. Young readers are introduced to new concepts, facts, ideas, and vocabulary.

Tips for Reading Nonfiction with Young Readers

Talk about Nonfiction
Begin by explaining that nonfiction books give us information that is true. The book will be organized around a specific topic or idea, and we may learn new facts through reading.

Look at the Parts
Most nonfiction books have helpful features. Our *Little Mitchie* titles include color photographs and graphic aids, a table of contents, a glossary, and an index. Share the purpose of these features with your reader.

Color Photos and Graphic Aids
A lot of information can be found by "reading" photos, charts, maps, and other graphic aids found within nonfiction texts. Help your reader learn more about the different ways information can be displayed.

Table of Contents
Located at the front of the book, this list shows the big ideas within the text and the page numbers where they can be found.

Glossary
Located at the back of the book, the glossary defines key words and phrases that are related to the topic. These words and phrases can be found in the text in colored type.

Index
Located at the back of the book, an index is an alphabetical list of topics and the page numbers where they can be found.

With a little help and guidance about reading nonfiction, you can feel good about introducing a young reader to the world of *Little Mitchie* nonfiction books.

Mitchell Lane
PUBLISHERS

2001 SW 31st Avenue
Hallandale, FL 33009
www.mitchelllanepub.com

Copyright © 2025 by Mitchell Lane Publishers. All rights reserved. No part of this book may be reproduced without written permission from the publisher. Printed and bound in the United States of America.

First Edition, 2025.

Author: Meg Greve
Designer: Rhea Magaro
Editor: Madison Greve

Names/credits:
Title: Digging Up Dinosaur Fossils in North America / by Meg Greve
Description: Hallandale, FL : Mitchell Lane Publishers, [2025]

Series: Digging Up Dinosaur Fossils
Library bound ISBN: 979-8-89260-242-6
Paperback ISBN: 979-8-89260-419-2
eBook ISBN: 979-8-89260-245-7

Little Mitchie is an imprint of Mitchell Lane Publishers.

PHOTO CREDITS
Shutterstock: Warpaint, cover, 1, 13; Colorcocktail, cover, 1 (sign); Matis75, 3; Aust28, 4, 6, 9, 11, 13, 15, 17, 18, 20, 23; Noiel, 5; Gorodenkoff, 6-7; Orla, 8-9, 18-19; MattL_Images, 10-11; rodos studio FERHAT CINAR, 12-13; Daniel Eskridge, 14-15, 16-17; algre, 14-15; kikujungboy CC, 20-21

Contents

When Dinosaurs Ruled the Land	4
Meat for Dinner? Meet the Carnivores!	9
More Plants for the Herbivores, Please!	15
Where Did the Dinosaurs Live?	22
Interesting Facts	23
Spotlight On: Sue Hendricks	23
Glossary	24
Index	24
Further Reading	24
On the Internet	24

When Dinosaurs Ruled the Land

The earth trembles. Small animals scatter. The mighty Tyrannosaurus snatches one of the animals with its huge jaw. This was North America before it was a **continent**. This was the time of the dinosaurs!

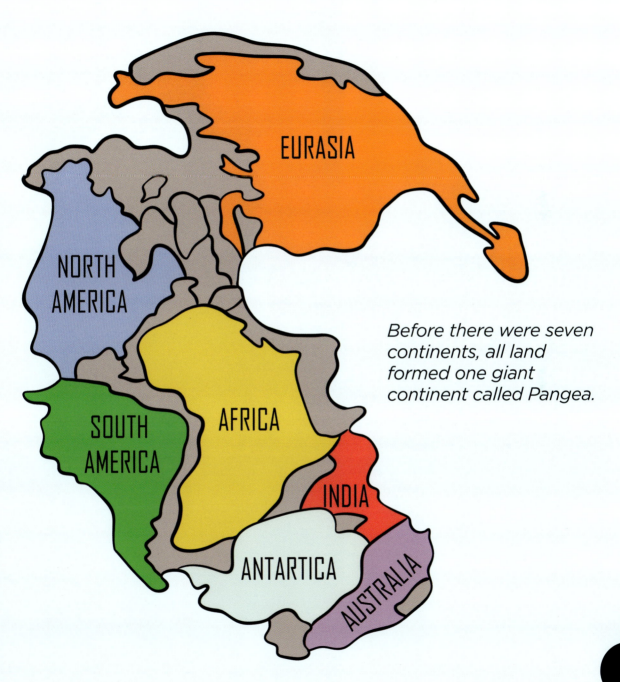

Before there were seven continents, all land formed one giant continent called Pangea.

More than 200 million years ago, long before humans, dinosaurs ruled the earth. How do we know? We found their **fossils**! Paleontologists study fossils to learn how dinosaurs lived.

DINO DETAILS: Meat-eating dinosaurs used super sharp teeth to tear their food.

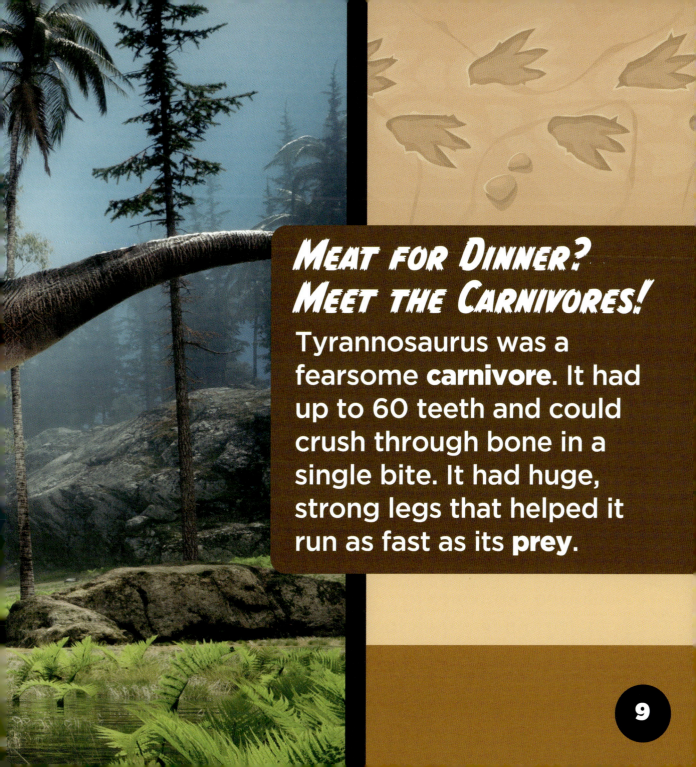

Meat for Dinner? Meet the Carnivores!

Tyrannosaurus was a fearsome **carnivore**. It had up to 60 teeth and could crush through bone in a single bite. It had huge, strong legs that helped it run as fast as its **prey**.

DINO DETAILS:
Sharp teeth and claws allowed carnivores to snatch and tear their food.

Allosaurus had a huge skull that was not very heavy. Even though it was not fast, it could bring down some very big plant-eating dinosaurs.

DINO DETAILS:
A long tail helped dinosaurs keep their balance while they hunted.

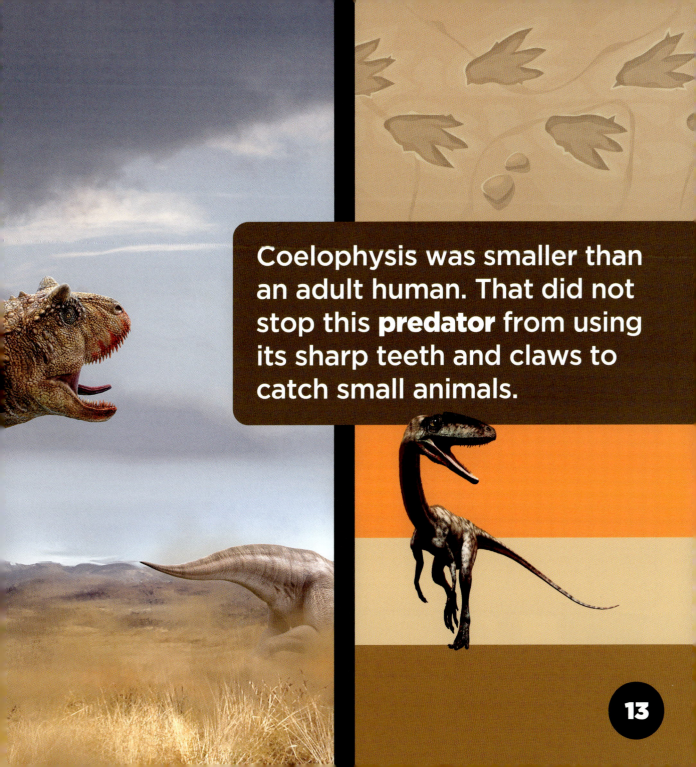

Coelophysis was smaller than an adult human. That did not stop this **predator** from using its sharp teeth and claws to catch small animals.

DINO DETAILS:
Diplodocus was about 104 feet (32 meters) long. That is about the length of a trailer on a truck!

More Plants for the Herbivores, Please!

Diplodocus may have been a plant-eating **herbivore**, but its size might scare you anyway! It had teeth shaped like pegs that were perfect for chewing leaves on the tops of tall trees.

DINO DETAILS: Stegosaurus had a beak to tear away plants, but it did not have teeth to chew.

Stegosaurus had big, strong plates along its back. But it protected itself with sharp spikes at the end of its tail. One huge swing could keep away most predators.

Ankylosaurus was covered in thick, bony plates. It had a huge club at the end of its tail. This was enough to keep away predators while eating plants low to the ground.

DINO DETAILS:
Most plant-eating dinosaurs did not have strong teeth or claws. They relied on their thick skin and sharp spikes to keep them safe.

Dinosaurs may have lived millions of years ago, but they may still seem alive to us now. New fossils are found every day. They tell the story of the time when dinosaurs ruled Earth.

Where Did the Dinosaurs Live?

More than 300 different dinosaur fossils have been found in North America. These are just a few!

- **Tyrannosaurus:** Montana, North Dakota, South Dakota, Texas, Wyoming, Montana, Colorado, New Mexico, Alberta
- **Allosaurus:** Colorado, Utah, Wyoming, Montana
- **Coelophysis:** Texas and New Mexico
- **Diplodocus:** Colorado, Utah, Montana, Wyoming
- **Stegosaurus:** Colorado, Utah, Wyoming
- **Ankylosaurus:** Montana

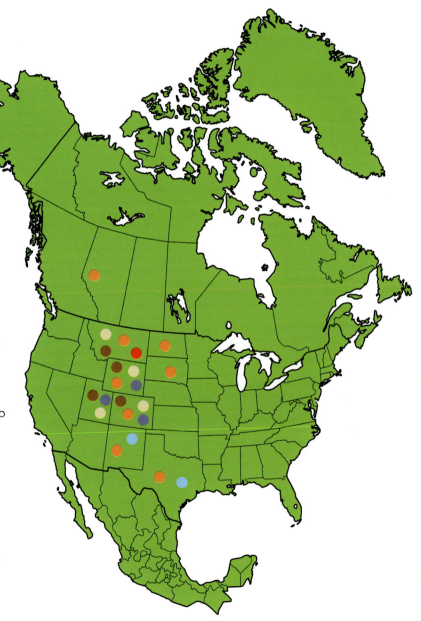

Interesting Facts

- The word dinosaur means "terrible lizard."
- Many dinosaurs may have been covered in feathers.
- About 66 million years ago, a huge asteroid crashed into Earth that killed off all dinosaurs except for birds.
- Today's birds are related to dinosaurs.
- Dinosaurs first appeared on Earth about 252 million years ago.

Spotlight On: Sue Hendrickson

Sue Hendrickson is a paleontologist and scientist. In 1990, she was digging for fossils in South Dakota when she saw a bone sticking out of a hill. She kept digging and a team of people joined her. The bones belonged to a Tyrannosaurus rex! It is the largest fossil ever found. The bones were put on display and given the name of Sue.

Glossary

carnivore (KAR-ni-vor):
A meat-eating animal

continent (KON-tin-ent):
One of the seven largest pieces of land on Earth

fossils (FAH-suhls):
Rock that forms after a living thing is preserved in the earth

herbivore (ER-buh-vor):
A plant-eating animal

predator (PRE-duh-ter):
An animal that hunts other animals for food

prey (pray):
Animals hunted and eaten by other animals

Index

Allosaurus 11, 22
Ankylosaurus 18, 22
Coelophysis 13, 22
Diplodocus 14, 15, 22
fossils 6, 20, 22, 23
North America 4, 22
paleontologist(s) 6, 23
Stegosaurus 16, 17, 22
Tyrannosaurus 4, 9, 22, 23

Further Reading

Barker, Chris Dr. and Riley Black. *Dinosaur Knowledge Genius!*. Dallas, TX: Brown Books Publishing Group, 2021.

Lowery, Mike. *Everything Awesome About Dangerous Dinosaurs*. New York, NY: Scholastic, 2023.

Yang, Yang. *The Secrets of Dinosaurs*. Dallas, TX: Brown Books Publishing Group, 2021.

On the Internet

Meet Some Deadly Dinos!
https://www.natgeokids.com/uk/discover/animals/prehistoric-animals/meet-some-deadly-dinos/
Learn lots of facts about dinosaurs that lived all over the world.

Dinosaurs: Tour a Dinosaur Lab
https://sciencetrek.org/topics/dinosaurs
Watch a tour of a dinosaur lab and learn facts about dinosaurs.